CELIBACY
After
SEX

A 50-Day Celibacy Journal Encouraging Couples
To Love God's Way

Stephan H. Blount & Alexis D. Jones

CELIBACY *After* SEX

Copyright © 2018

Unless otherwise noted, Scripture quotations are from The King James Version of the Bible.

ISBN 13: 9781973916833

DEDICATION

This book is dedicated to all couples.

We pray that our testimony blesses your lives and encourages you to trust in God's timing.

CELIBACY *After* SEX

THANK YOU

To all of our family, friends and supporters. We thank you for your support and love during our journey.

Truly this book has been a labor of love but, more importantly, submission of our will to God's. Although our commitment has not always been easy, we rest assured that it will eternally be worth it.

CELIBACY *After* SEX

Table of Contents

INTRODUCTION: WHY ARE WE HERE?

We exist because God desired reciprocal love, which is why He created man in His own image. He wanted us to get to know Him, love Him and fellowship with Him. He created Adam and Eve with the power of free will. And that is when the trouble began.

God was very pleased with Adam and Eve: they did all that He created them to do—lived in a perfect world, fellowshipped with and honored the perfect creator. But because they had free will, Adam and Eve had the choice to reject or to love Him. We have that same choice today.

Most blame Satan for lying to and confusing them, but it was their fatal decision that caused Adam and Eve to sin and thereby lose their fellowship with God. The cost was even greater: sin was introduced to mankind. The two dishonored God by trying to imitate Him through Satan's manipulation.

The same holds true for us today. We have free will, but every choice either demonstrates that we **reject** Him or **love** Him. In theory, it is as simple as that.

You may ask: *So why does God tell us what we can and cannot do?* If every choice is a *life or death* decision, and He knew we would often make the wrong one, why would God give us free will? If he knows that it's hard for us to avoid sinning, why does He make so many laws that punish us?

Think of it this way: as a parent, would you want your children to respond as robots or would you rather train and instruct them in the way they should go and leave them to make the best decision? Even if they made a wrong choice, it would be a lesson learned and one that you hope would stir them back in the right direction. God is the same way.

God's laws were not created to punish or restrict us from having fun. He simply wants to protect and guide us through life and, if we obey Him, we will learn that He will never fail us. Although we live with the consequences of sin, God blesses us with the gift of His grace. He made the ultimate sacrifice, offering up his son Jesus, to afford us the opportunity to choose to live for Him every single day.

CAUTION: We also have the choice to live against Him. Choose wisely.

Like a parent, God knows that it's hard to avoid sinning. He knew long before today that sin would be the norm and that our flesh constantly wars with the spirit. However, once we give our lives over to Christ, God's spirit dwells on the inside of us giving us the power to win the war through prayer and supplication. It all comes down to LOVE.

> **1 JOHN 4:8** He that loveth not knoweth not god; for **god is love**.

As sons and daughters of Christ, we should have a sound and hearty desire to do His will. Anything that appears to be love but contradicts our Creator's law is not the kind of relationship God intended for us to have. Because we are children of the Most High, we want to love and be loved because of who we are and whom we serve, not because of what we provide sexually. We don't want to be so hooked on sex and pleasing our partner that we forget to serve God with our whole heart, mind, body and soul.

CELIBACY *After* SEX

The thrill of instant gratification will cause us to disobey God by following the world and not the will of our Lord and Savior. This is what happened with Adam and Eve and look at the impact it had on our world even centuries later. Fornication is arguably one of the hardest sins to shake and there is no pretty way to clean up a big mess. For Stephan and me, it took faith, hard work and rededication to turn our love life around. We weren't trying to be *super spiritual, super saved* or *religious*. We are simply two people that love God, prayed and then waited until He answered. What He revealed to us is found in the pages of this book.

CELIBACY *After* SEX will guide you through 50 days of what we consider our "turnaround season." Hopefully, the path we chose to correct the errors we made in the early stage of our relationship will be a great source of help for you. Please keep your hearts and minds open to what God is doing in this season and what He is saying to you. We know that He will bless you just as He has blessed us.

We pray that our words and testimonies shared in this book will speak to your soul and help you approach God's desired change for your life and relationship. We hope that you will join together in your pursuit to please God with full boldness and confidence.

Remember, God does not expect us to be perfect, He just wants a relationship with us. As long as we:

1. Admit that we are sinners and repent,

2. Believe that Jesus is God's son AND

3. Confess our faith in Jesus Christ as Lord and Savior and turn away from sin…

…we will be okay.

FOCUS AND DISCIPLINE

Let's start with a pill that is bitter for many of us to swallow:

CELIBACY is one of the most important acts of spiritual growth in preparation for a healthy relationship & successful marriage.

It's difficult to check your heart and measure the love you have for your significant other while your vision is clouded with lust and fornication. How can we even pray for clarity about a situation when we aren't keeping God's commandments?

We get into these relationships with people and end up in a world of mess, then call on Jesus to bail us out of a situation we wouldn't be in if we had been obedient. When we commit acts against His divine law, we are pushed further and further away from our purpose.

Putting our fleshly desires to rest and focusing on God will give us discipline and discernment. Focusing on Jesus will give us the ability to transfer the energy that we once gave to sex over to His kingdom. Even if we have met the man or woman whom God created for us, we can ruin it by being disobedient. We might end up destroying our *good thing* by making poor decisions and willful acts of disobedience.

Continuing to have sex outside of marriage is to continue to challenge God. This is no simple act of *just a vice* or *God knows my heart.* Sex outside of marriage leads to suffering for us and our children, present and future. Many of us are products of broken homes and have experienced things that God never intended for us to because of our parents' willful acts of disobedience. Concentrating on God and being disciplined will bring us great fruit in our relationships as well as prosperity in our future.

God is calling us to come out of the world and be separated. This is for our own good. Fornication is dangerous and it isn't worth the few minutes of pleasure that can lead to a lifetime of pain. The results of sin do not bring glory and honor to God at all.

1 THESSALONIANS 4: 3 For this is the will of God, even your sanctification, that ye should abstain from fornication:

4 That every one of you should know how to possess his vessel in sanctification and honour;

5 Not in the lust of concupiscence, even as the Gentiles which know not God:

WHAT IS *FORNICATION*?

There is no sense in sharing God's revelation if we don't have a clear understanding first. Many families and even churches shy away from discussions of sex in any form.

So let's define what fornication[1] really is, and in all forms, so you can begin your journey with clarity:

FORNICATION (Merriam-Webster):

consensual sexual intercourse between two persons not married to each other.

Some of you might be thinking, *Okay, so we can't have sex. Got it.* As hard as that can be, simply abstaining from physical sex is not all that's required. And, honestly, this is the same conversation we need to have with many of our youth.

Too many times, children are being told to abstain from sex, but not other forms of sex such as oral and anal. There are females that are "protecting their virginity" but think it's okay to engage in oral and anal sex. Many Christians who say they are celibate also engage in oral sex, believing this is not fornication or it is the lesser of two evils. The reality is neither is pleasing to God.

---

[1] fornication. 2019. In *Merriam-Webster.com.* Retrieved January 21, 2019, from https://www.merriam-webster.com/dictionary/fornication.

If you review the above definition of fornication, it mentions *sexual intercourse* (Merriam-Webster, 2019)[2]:

SEXUAL INTERCOURSE (Merriam-Webster):

1: heterosexual intercourse involving penetration of the vagina by the penis

2: intercourse (such as anal or oral intercourse) that does not involve penetration of the vagina by the penis

---

Did you catch that? Don't be ashamed if you read any of this and it's the first time you've seen it.

For clarity, ALL sex outside of marriage is FORBIDDEN as well as sexually immoral conduct, which includes oral, anal and sexual penetration and masturbation. It doesn't matter whether masturbation is done privately or in the presence of another, these practices are contrary to God's instructions to keep our temples honorable, holy and avoiding lust.

People often argue that God wouldn't give you sexual urges and desires and then demand that you wait to act on them. Think of it this way: you can buy a car but there are laws of the land that say you must have a driver's license or permit and car insurance before driving. If caught driving without these things, you not only put your life and the lives of others in danger, you also risk losing your privileges.

---

[2] fornication. 2019. In *Merriam-Webster.com*. Retrieved January 21, 2019, from https://www.merriam-webster.com/dictionary/sexual intercourse.

CELIBACY *After* SEX

Rules and regulations are established for your safety and to protect the lives of others. The same is true, even more so, when it comes to God and his commandments/directives.

Now that you have clarity, you can fulfill God's word.

DAY 1

DAY 1

Stephan:

There have been many "Day 1's" for Alexis and me on the journey of celibacy, especially since we initially took the journey lightly. We weren't focusing on the Word or setting time aside to pray and invite God on the journey with us. We thought we could do it alone, but we quickly realized that sheer willpower could never be strong enough without the help of Jesus Christ. After surrendering our desires unto the Lord, reading the Bible and praying, we were successful.

Making this commitment to God helped me grow spiritually as a man and as a partner. Although I am journaling and making this life change with Alexis, I enjoy alone time with the Lord. It isn't always necessary to pray and read the Bible as a couple. Of course, I want God's very best for both of us, but my ultimate goal is to continue building a personal relationship with God. The result of my personal relationship with God will greatly impact our relationship.

God ordained us men to one day become the head of the house (Ephesians 5:22–33). We won't be able to do that successfully if we don't submit to Him first and be good examples of His Word prior to becoming husbands.

Focusing on His law and keeping His commandments while single will make the transition as the head of the house easier. I urge you to devote time to God and keep your partner lifted in prayer during this time of transition.

DAY 1

Alexis:

During this turning point in your relationship, you must shift your focus to God. We have to literally sit at the feet of Jesus and pray for focus, direction and discipline. Sis, it is going to get extremely difficult to feed your spirit and resist your flesh. At this point, you've acknowledged what is right and what is wrong, but it is so easy to jump back into the routine that you are most comfortable with.

The devil is going to be busy throughout this season of your life. Satan is going to try to attack your mind and try to distract you. You are going to think about sex–you are going to think about how good it made you feel and how close you felt to your significant other while the two of you were having sex (committing fornication). But you have to remember that you've made it through the storm and God has you in the palm of His hand. You are stronger and wiser than you were at that point in your relationship. So when Satan interrupts your thoughts with what used to be "good times," put a praise on it and thank God for deliverance.

I'll be honest: sometimes I find myself reminiscing on the past and how good sex with Stephan was. When this happens, I analyze what really occurred from a spiritual perspective vs. my natural eye. I remind myself that beneath all of the pleasure, Stephan and I were wrong and willfully chose to sin against God. We were no strangers to the word so we knew better. Just like Adam and Eve, we chose to make a deadly decision knowing that all sin is a type of death. And we risked our eternal lives by engaging in a deadly practice over and over again.

To say you know God is a powerful statement, so I'll reiterate:

We knew God when we were having sex, but we ignored Him and continued to do what we wanted to do.

For a while, that guilt followed me because I could identify the times when I heard God's voice telling me to stop, but I kept going. My actions haunted me until I was able to truly ask God for forgiveness and focus on what He wanted me to do now, even if that meant leaving Stephan.

And so can you.

DAY 2

DAY 2

Stephan:

Changing your routine will break the barrier between your flesh and your faith and help you to be celibate.

Adding devotional time to your daily schedule and documenting your journey will provide an outlet to express and overcome challenges and downfalls. Of course, some days will be more thought-provoking than others, but reflecting on easier days gives you a push, especially as you are reading your own words. Changing your routine and inviting the spirit of expectancy enhances the likelihood of being successful.

Expect to be successful, expect to overcome temptation and expect to learn and grow in Christ. There are several activities that you can devote more of your time to that will keep your mind off of sex. Join an organization, invest more time in a friend or sibling, attend Bible study or pick up extra shifts at work. Idle time is the devil's playground (Proverbs 16:27–29), therefore, I encourage you to stay occupied. Adapting to a routine change will take patience, focus and discipline, but with teamwork and prayer, your journey will be easier.

New Activities List:

_____   _____

_____   _____

_____   _____

_____   _____

DAY 2

Alexis:

Don't forget to celebrate your wins.

Making it through one day of not having sex is an accomplishment. You are celibate, praise God! You've acknowledged that you are worth being loved the right way and, most of all, God is proud of you. Your renewed passion for pleasing Him and representing His kingdom is amazing.

At this point, it is important to change your routine. Stephan and I were locked in a pattern of sin because we never altered our way of living. It was hard to take sex off the table when I dressed in revealing clothes for date nights or walked around in a towel after taking a shower. How could I expect Stephan to be strong if I was exciting his flesh with revealing tops, tight dresses and prancing around him in nothing but a towel?

Changing your way of life isn't going to be easy, but it will be worth it. Always remember that you can do all things through Jesus Christ who strengthens you (Philippians 4:13).

What Activities do you need to Change?

_____   _____

_____   _____

_____   _____

_____   _____

DAY 3

DAY 3

Stephan:

Today will be another testament to strong faith and patience whether it's celibacy, working or being in school. The same is true of every single day.

There are so many things that the devil tries to use to distract us, from social media and music to pornography. All of these diversions are in place to remove our focus from God.

I do believe that for some, it may be harder than others to stay dedicated to a true walk with Christ. Sometimes I struggle with a lack of focus, but I pray every day for wisdom and to be more like Christ and less like the world.

What are some of the ways Satan uses to distract you, especially in your journey of celibacy?

_____

_____

_____

_____

_____

_____

DAY 3

Alexis:

I love to pray for Stephan and his strength on this journey. It is so easy for me to go into praise mode for the man who is willing to chase God with me.

Say a special prayer for your future husband and ask God to continue to strengthen both of you while traveling on this journey that is often difficult and lonely.

> *God, I lift my future husband to You and I pray for his strength, obedience and wisdom. I pray that he continues to seek You and strive to please You and love You with all of his heart, soul, mind and strength (Mark 12:30, 1 Samuel 16:7). Keep him covered, oh God, physically and mentally.*
>
> *When times get tough, remind him that You are in control. I thank you for Your grace and unwavering favor over our lives. I trust that you are with us, now and forever. In your son Jesus' name . . . Amen!*

What are some areas you need to pray for your future spouse in?

_____   _____

_____   _____

_____   _____

_____   _____

DAY 4

DAY 4

Stephan:

Finding different things to do outside of the bedroom can be beneficial during the transitional stage of breaking free from fornication.

Alexis and I found time to go to the movies and embrace each other without feeling the need to sin. This discovery alone makes me give thanks to God.

To God be the glory. I am able to take His many blessings and enjoy them with the woman I love. God has been so good to me (to us).

I believe that setting ground rules makes the transition to celibacy easier. I'm attracted to Alexis as I'm sure you are attracted to your significant other, however, I think it is important for Alexis to dress respectfully as to not tempt me. I like her to avoid showing cleavage and wearing short/tight dresses.

If you know that the way your woman dresses makes you lust after fornication, then respectfully ask her to help you by following somewhat of a "dress code." Take this time to work together and devise standards that work best for both of you.

As men, we have to continue asking God for strength to live by His words. Today I am setting a goal for myself to incorporate the Bible in my writing, dissect the scriptures and better apply them to my life (Psalms 119:105).

DAY 4

Alexis:

We must live in accordance with what the Bible has declared to be true. In the midst of this life change, we have to remember all that God has promised us as a result of our obedience.

It's important to guard your relationship with prayer and stand on the word of God while transitioning to a new state of being.

Remember that everyone can't travel with the two of you as you are fighting sin and turning your lives around. Ungodly friendships can be toxic during this season. I'm not suggesting that you shut the door on people who still have sex with their significant others. I'm saying that you don't need negative feedback from those who don't agree with your decision.

I remember telling a loved one that Stephan and I were celibate and we weren't having sex until marriage. She went on and on about *how hard it is to find a good black man* and how I was *crazy as hell*. She told me that I needed to *do what I needed to do to keep my man*.

I remember being extremely upset. Of course, those thoughts crossed my mind, but I was confident in what the Lord was doing in our relationship and I didn't want to hear those words from someone who I considered to be a close friend. I was left with no other choice but to distance myself from her.

Food for Thought: I did not distance myself from her as a form of retaliation or hurt, but simply because we did not share the same beliefs. No, I am not suggesting that you cut off all those who live contrary lifestyles, but you must be careful with your close relationships and who you allow to feed your spirit.

The friend I mentioned viewed obedience as optional for her and our lifestyles differed significantly. I didn't need her planting bad seeds in my life and trying to deter me from my purpose. Remember, this is the same type of behavior that Satan illustrated in the Garden of Eden.

Sis, you are on your way to becoming a wife. In God's timing, you'll be a fiancée. We have to start guarding our dwelling now (Titus 2:3–5). That begins by declaring peace in your relationship and dismissing any foul friendships or conversations that come against your relationship and, most of all, the Word of God.

DAY 5

DAY 5

Stephan:

T hings can change instantaneously. Today I needed the Lord to give me strength because I was weak. In the event that you experience weakness, pray. Pray immediately, constantly and without ceasing:

Thank You, God, for life, health and strength. Lord, I need You right now! I am trying to be more like You. I am not perfect and there are things You and I both know I struggle with. I feel tempted, Lord, but give me strength, God. Strengthen my mind, my heart and my soul.

Please help keep my mind focused on You and doing the right things. Give me the discernment to recognize triggers that may cause me to falter and fornicate. I need Your direction, God, to lead me to the right people who can encourage me in doing Your will.

I pray for Alexis as well, God. Continue to encourage her and give her strength on our journey together. Now, God, I ask You to have mercy on me and forgive me for all of my sins. In Your loving and Holy name, I pray, Amen.

DAY 5

Alexis:

I would agree that having sex was one of the most prominent ways of expressing love in our relationship. It wasn't the only way, but it was an enjoyable way to "show love." I'd have to disagree now, though, because disrespecting our Heavenly Father is not a representation of true love. And, if we look beyond the fleshly, temporal pleasure, there is nothing pleasurable about spending life in eternal damnation.

Today, I believe abstaining from sex shows Stephan that I really love him and the scripture below proves it:

GALATIONS 5:13 For, brethren, ye have been called unto liberty; only use not liberty for an occasion to the flesh, but by love serve one another.

14 For all the law is fulfilled in one word, even in this; Thou shalt love thy neighbour as thyself.

15 But if ye bite and devour one another, take heed that ye be not consumed one of another.

16 This I say then, Walk in the Spirit, and ye shall not fulfil the lust of the flesh.

17 For the flesh lusteth against the Spirit, and the Spirit against the flesh: and these are contrary the one to the other: so that ye cannot do the things that ye would.

If you truly love someone, would you set them up for failure or harm? Would you willingly stand by and watch them be hurt, hurt themselves or go down to a path of destruction? Of course not! But, unfortunately, we often don't see fornication as the same. In fact, it is even worse!

Fornication is an invitation of entrapment and danger. You not only hurt yourself, but you create the perfect environment for those who join you to also be hurt eternally. You are not only digging a hole for them to fall in, but you're pushing them in and jumping right behind them! Sounds familiar? That is what Satan did with Adam and Eve.

Do you know how many people struggle today from past sexual partners? Forget sexually transmitted diseases or unwanted pregnancies, I'm referring to soul ties. In God's perfect plan, sex was created for the never-ending bond of marriage between a man and a woman. Just because sin entered the world and we often choose to go outside of His natural order, does not mean the bond/tie was destroyed.

Too many women and men cannot seem to shake that last relationship, even though they know the person was not good for them. He or she can't seem to "let go" or "move on" from the relationship that no longer exists. That is because their soul has meshed with that person, and many of the spirits that person entertained sexually, although the relationship has ended.

Love God first and love your future spouse second. Be crafty in both your methods on how to avoid fornication as well as show your love for your partner. I challenge you to find a way to let your significant other know that you appreciate their commitment to you and the Lord in its purest and innocent form.

DAY 6

DAY 6

Stephan:

S ometimes sex is classified as a stress reliever. Alexis and I are at two different stages in life, but sex was our common outlet to release stress and to relax. Today I felt like Alexis' anxiety was at an all-time high due to the stress of school.

I couldn't let her frustration drive us into the bedroom and let the devil ride (literally).

Instead, we shifted our focus on other things. We started watching a new series on Netflix that struck both of our interests as current and potential healthcare professionals. I also encouraged her to spend more time verbally communicating her thoughts and feelings to me. Shutting me out of issues does not bode for a healthy relationship and, quite frankly, most times it causes both parties to become frustrated. So, fellas, set time aside to listen to your ladies, even when you feel her issues are minute in the grand scheme of things. This goes a long way in a successful relationship as well: we cannot lead our household if we do not know how to listen to the problems of our spouse.

If you experience a slip in communication, or just end up frustrated after a demanding day at work or school, I suggest you treat it like a challenge. Develop alternatives to strengthen your relationship and relieve stress, rather than falling back into the same cycle you desire to grow from.

Today I began a seven-day devotional time praying for my relationship and all of the future blessings I would like to see.

DAY 6

Alexis:

It's so beautiful to know that the value of your relationship comes from Christ. You'll always know that what's between your legs isn't what kept your man around and what's between another woman's legs won't make him leave.

A man who is grounded in the Word and fears God is a man to be praised. There's a special feeling inside when you know your guy loves you enough to repent, ask God for forgiveness and abstain from sex until marriage.

Prayer:

Oh God, I thank You for breaking all ungodly soul ties with men in my past. I cast out every spirit of lust, in the name of Jesus. I declare that I am loosed from any spirit of perversion and unfaithfulness, right now, in the name of Jesus. I bind every stronghold and loose the chains of every generational curse right now, God. I have open arms and receive purity and holiness in my heart. Amen.

DAY 7

DAY 7

Stephan:

God has called and chosen you to make this change and, despite all that could've kept you bound to sin, you did it! Completing your first week of celibacy is no small accomplishment, especially if you and your partner are anything like Alexis and I used to be. This is a testament to your dedication and willingness to change.

Remaining celibate and serving God is a spiritual gift. Continue to press on and be true to your calling. We aren't on this journey by mistake. We are here because obedience will align us with our purpose. This commitment will shape us and build us in ways that we would have never imagined.

Thankfully, I feel a positive difference in my health overall. I pray that you can also identify changes in your life, regardless if you consider it to be significant. We have to thank God for all that is happening and not take his blessings for granted.

DAY 7

Alexis:

B eing sensitive to God's voice is important for success on this celibacy journey, especially during the early stages. We need to be able to recognize when God is telling us something or when He is saying yes. Sometimes we won't get a response as soon as we want, but I promise you that God is always on time.

When God makes Himself recognizable to you, it is imperative that you act promptly on His spiritual impressions and that you're obedient to whatever He is saying, even if it isn't what you want to hear.

Congratulations on completing one week of celibacy. Stephan and I celebrate each week like an anniversary. It's so easy to celebrate when I think of all the hell that we've avoided by being obedient to God.

Remember to be selective about whom you share your triumphs or tribulations with—not everyone is living to please God. If people don't know Jesus, they don't know or appreciate your struggle and sacrifice.

What are some of your celebrations in your completed one week of celibacy?

(Don't forget to count what you think of as small.)

HIS	HER
_____	_____
_____	_____
_____	_____
_____	_____
_____	_____
_____	_____
_____	_____

VISION

The love of God truly creates wholeness. If you're feeling discouraged about waiting to have sex until marriage, please know that you are not alone. It's hard to cut sex off after you've experienced it and for an extended period (two years for us).

When times get tough, we encourage you to reread your journal entries from last week and focus on the vision that you and your partner have for your relationship (soon to be marriage). Really get into it and take it seriously, because God will bless the two of you with favor and unconditional love for one another.

Before you know it, you'll be married. God is changing you into the best version of yourself that you can be. This transition will benefit both of you significantly. Take some time to set standards and goals for your relationship.

Although this journey is extremely serious, it is also FUN. Do your part to make it exciting and enjoyable. Own your walk and make it unique to fit the bond between you and your love. Alexis and I have so much fun planning our wedding, discussing finances and even planning our engagement party.

DAY 8

DAY 8

Stephan:

My faith is so big concerning this journey that it doesn't even make sense. I am motivated and excited about moving forward.

I believe Alexis is getting frustrated and a little annoyed, but that's okay because I am here to encourage her and pray her through. I appreciate her transparency and willingness to stay committed, but I want her to keep her faith strong.

She gets overwhelmed and frustrated with trying to perfect all of her weak areas all at once. She's very analytical and, even though she knows that we are all a work in progress, she still expects to change overnight. My prayer for her today is that she will realize who she's serving. I'm reminding her that God will give her peace for keeping His commands and that He will see her through (Proverbs 3:1–2).

DAY 8

Alexis:

I would agree that it is slightly difficult to stop having sex with someone whom you feel like God created to be your husband. I am really learning how to depend on God during this time because I was starting to move with haste.

Sis, I was ready to go to the courthouse because I did not want to be celibate for five years. I remember reading that it is better to marry than to burn with lust (1 Corinthians 7:9). So I built the courage to ask Stephan if he wanted to go get married at the courthouse. He told me no and explained why he felt that going through this process was good for us.

Frustrated and upset, I asked him when we were getting married. (Mind you, we had already discussed this several times.) Stephan has always been transparent about his plans with me but, of course, he couldn't move on anything without confiding in the Lord. But even after talking to Stephan, I was no longer praying for strength and direction. I was praying to rush getting hitched.

Our relationship needs to go through the waiting stage. Just because marriage is the way out of celibacy doesn't mean that we are ordained to take it. After all, what was I rushing for? We had already done it. I was acting like an addict and I was a hot mess. If Stephan had entertained my foolishness, I would've married with haste. So I thank God for His wisdom and patience.

When I feel anxious (Philippians 4:6–7), I pray and plan my Pinterest wedding. There is nothing wrong with getting prepared and creating a vision for your special day.

DAY 9

DAY 9

Stephan:

God knows our hearts: I believe that and I carry that thought with me every day. I am not the type of Christian who feels like I have to prove anything to anyone about my walk with God. I don't claim to be perfect and I never want to be so religious and self-righteous that I feel like I have to prove to people who I am.

Please don't confuse this with sharing your growth and what the Lord is doing in your life. 1 Chronicles 16:8 tells us to *give thanks to the Lord and make His deeds known to the people*, but be sure to do it your way. Effective praise should always be sincere. Our worship shouldn't be for the world; it is all about our love for the One who has been good to us! God appreciates the reality of our praise and we owe it to Him.

People will recognize your growth just by being in your presence. Be who you are and everything else will flow. You don't have to post that you're celibate on social media. You don't even have to tell anyone. Take this time to embrace yourself and be authentic.

You don't have to do it as anyone else does it; dress it up and do it your way. As long as you are on one accord with God, you will be alright. We don't want to get too caught up in pleasing people, because it is not they who will judge us and advocate on our behalf before the Lord.

DAY 9

Alexis:

I like to associate this change in my relationship as an avenue to build standards and present expectations to Stephan that I'd like to carry into our marriage. During this stage of celibacy and focusing on your vision, please don't get so wrapped up in planning your wedding that you forget about the marriage. It's very easy to do when you start pinning all those pretty dresses and taking note of the best venues in town.

Don't get comfortable with discussing getting married once or twice with your future husband and think that's enough. Realize that change is happening. We have to stay on one accord because our thought process will shift regularly. You should not feel the same way about marriage that you felt last month or even last week. You should be developing a new thought process concerning what's to come in your courtship.

Think about the greatness that God has in store as the reward for your obedience. It's time to get busy and create a five-year plan. I encourage you to include finances, ministries and everything that you want God to do in your life. Please share this idea with your man and speak life over this plan. If it is God's will and you're in alignment, it will be done!

DAY 10

DAY 10

Stephan:

Today I feel led to share a special prayer on faith/healing.

God, I thank You for waking me up in my right mind.

I thank You for putting a roof over my head, clothes on my back and food on my table. Lord, I thank You for having so many examples of Godly women and men in my family who have spent many nights praying for and with me. Today, God, I just ask that You continue to show me the way You want me to go. Lord, if it is not You, I do not want to be part of it.

I am so encouraged and have no one but You to thank for my progress. Now, Lord, I ask that You heal each one of my loved ones and friends. Even if they do not know that their bodies or minds are under attack by the enemy, heal them now God. I am believing You will remove cancer, deal with depression, heal those with HIV, cancel thoughts of suicide and take care of any other needs of Your people. Have Your way, God, in my life as well as in Alexis' life. Let us continue to be the Godly couple You called us to be.

I believe You for the increase, God, not just financially, but also in wisdom and strength. I declare that every wicked attack from the enemy to distract or destroy what you have planned is canceled right now. Devil, you lose yet again! In Jesus's name, I pray, Amen.

DAY 10

Alexis:

Making a timeline isn't fun when you're reading a history book and turning it in for a grade. We thought it may prove to be very beneficial to discuss our five-year plan aloud. Make sure your plans include God.

Remember that marriage includes three (God, man and woman), not two. You are pushing yourselves to be leaders of His kingdom and your story will change lives and win souls. Documenting your vision for your relationship and life, in general, may prove very beneficial. It's nice to have something to look back on and share with your friends and family (Habakkuk 2:2).

DAY 11

DAY 11

Stephan:

God is the author of our lives, which means our love story has already been written. We don't have to force anything. There is no blueprint for your relationship. Everything should be authentic and that will come easily if we put our trust in God.

It's always good to seek advice and discuss topics with friends, but we have to make sure we are giving reverence to God in all that we do. Long before we make a decision, God already knows what the right one is. Therefore, when we get to the point where we are seriously thinking about marriage, it is important that we pray and are led by the Holy Spirit. We will find great comfort in our lives by letting God lead us to our destiny. We can save ourselves from pain and disappointment if we stop trying to make our dreams His will for our lives.

DAY 11

Alexis:

Prior to dating Stephan, I was in a terrible relationship. God clearly wasn't in the midst of that mess and I knew it. Once I finally closed that door, Stephan and I became friends, but we weren't communicating regularly. He was literally just a guy I knew from pharmacy school, nothing more and nothing less.

I remember desperately crying out to God and asking Him to fulfill the desires of my heart (Psalms 37:4). This is my favorite scripture because, after repeatedly praying and studying that scripture, I saw God move.

I could see His hand in my life and Him directing my path. It had been eight months since my breakup with my ex and I didn't want to rush into a new relationship without God's blessing. That heartbreak from my ex really took me through the fire. He intentionally bleached my clothes, chased after other women whom I knew and did everything under the sun to disrespect me. I lost weight; I was depressed; I was walking around as if no one loved me. But, at some point, I was reminded that God loved me.

I began devoting time every day to read my Bible and I even stopped cursing. Because I gave God a chance, I believe He healed me a lot faster than I thought possible. Without knowing what I was going through, Stephan checked in on me and we often talked about life, pharmacy school and several other topics. I began to like him and felt that God had given me the okay to move forward.

But as I became comfortable with Stephan and we began dating, I became a lukewarm Christian. Stephan even approached me a few times, toward the beginning of our relationship, stating that I had read my Bible lot more. But I would brush it off and kept doing me.

Putting Jesus on the back burner muted His voice in my life and He wasn't accessible to me when I needed direction. I was walking blindsided. I share this story with you in the hopes that you don't do what I did. I don't recommend that you welcome the Holy Spirit into your relationship and then shut Him out once things are going well. We need Christ throughout this journey. We need Him on the days when things are easier as well as the days when times get tough.

I truly believe that as women, we have the power to set the standard and we can stick to anything with God's help. Remember that our reward is in heaven and we will reap the benefits of being faithful servants (Matthew 25:23).

DAY 12

DAY 12

Stephan:

I believe God for so many things in my near future. I find myself devoting prayer time to thanking Him for the doors He has opened in my life as well as those He kept closed for my benefit. It is customary for me to thank God every time I begin a prayer, as I was taught to do as a child but, lately, I've been stuck on giving Him ALL the praise. He didn't have to do it, but He did! I do not deserve the amazing things God allows to happen in my life.

But favor ain't fair y'all!

I also have been praying for healing—healing loved ones from ailments in their bodies. Whether it is cancer, high blood pressure, diabetes, lupus, blood disorders, HIV, momentary muteness or any addictions, my unwavering faith and belief is that God is bad enough to heal our bodies at any millisecond. It doesn't always have to be medicine that cures our ailments. As a true believer in Christ, we must really maintain that "by His stripes we are healed" (Isaiah 53:5). No matter what a doctor's report or science may say, God has the final say in any matter. I just am trusting and believing Him that He is turning any negative situation 180-degrees for my good!

DAY 12

Alexis:

I think being saved is cool. It's like refusing to become your own problem and submitting to God and giving your life back to Him. I get excited when I think about what He has in store for me.

I know that this year, God is righting my wrongs and purifying what He intended to be good in the first place, all because I have agreed to die to my flesh and live in His will.

It's a powerful thing, my sister. I love you and I am so happy that I have you on this journey with me.

DAY 13

DAY 13

Stephan:

> **1 THESSALONIANS 2:13** says, "For this cause also thank we God without ceasing, because, when ye received the word of God which ye heard of us, ye received it not as the word of men, but as it is in truth, the word of God, which effectually worketh also in you that believe."

God is not a man that He should lie.

Therefore, I trust and believe in His Holy Word. All the promises He lays out for us as Christians are really for us!

It just feels awesome to be so encouraged, knowing that God is on my side when I walk into any unfamiliar territory—whether I'm at work, home or anywhere else. I can walk with the confidence that God will see me through any situation.

DAY 13

Alexis:

Secure the victory of waiting to have sex with your future husband until marriage. Keep your eyes on God and continue to walk in alignment because His will is so much better than our own. You'll be a happy wife because God's hand will be in your marriage. He will bring your vision to life with an abundance of peace and love because you kept His law.

> **PROVERBS 29:18** Where there is no vision, the people perish: but he that keepeth the law, happy is he.

DAY 14

DAY 14

Stephan:

Today I really wanted to go back to the basics. I felt I needed to "refresh" my mind or remind myself of what God expects from us as Christians.

I read from Exodus 20 today. For those of you who do not know, Exodus 20 is the first time the Ten Commandments are listed in the Bible.

Throughout this journey, I want to make sure that I am not only being celibate and not fornicating but also following the rest of God's commandments. That way I can become a better man of God, which is my ultimate goal.

I know I'm not exactly where God wants me to be, however, I am constantly trying to work on myself by praying and asking God to change my mindset. I am asking Him to give me a mind more like Jesus.

DAY 14

Alexis:

"No sin is greater than the other!"

This is one of the common phrases that people use as a crutch or comfort when they know they've done wrong. [Another one is "God knows my heart."] While I agree that both are true, we must consider the gravity of sin before we give ourselves a hall pass.

Even if telling a lie, cursing or disrespecting our parents seem minor, all are acts of sin. If we participate in any of those activities, we need to pray to God for deliverance. We must do better. These sins will push us further away from our destiny and so will sex.

For a long time, I told myself that there wasn't a big difference between me lying, cursing and having sex. I didn't see the need to intentionally correct my behavior because I had so many other things that I was doing that I knew weren't pleasing to God.

I didn't see it until one of my sisters in Christ told me that I was going to hell. She flat out told me, "You're going to hell." Harsh, right? Maybe a little extreme. But I thank God for her words.

I thank God that she told me I was wrong. I did not realize the power that sex carried. When magnifying the negative effects of sex, we are talking about babies, STDs, soul ties, death, heartbreak...the list goes on.

Don't get me wrong—when you dishonor your parents, your

days are cut short and being a reflection of God doesn't entail cursing or lying. But I wasn't cursing up a storm, because I acknowledged that it was wrong and I was trying to stop. I told white lies (also wrong), but I wasn't a dishonest person. However, when it came to sex...I had every excuse and reason why my sin wasn't that big of a deal.

I didn't see the need to stop, because I asked for forgiveness and God knew my heart, so I just knew He wasn't going to send me to hell. After all, as long as I completed my "ABCs" and my heart was in the right place, I was good. My spot in heaven was reserved and, since I am an upstanding citizen, I just knew Jesus would look out for me. He wasn't sending me to hell, not for having sex anyway. But I was so wrong.

My disrespect, hypocrisy and disobedience to God were all enough to earn me a one-way ticket to the pits of hell. Not because I had sex but because I didn't attempt to stop.

I charged every time I had sex on my forgiveness credit card and told God I'd pay Him back later with prayer after I asked Him for forgiveness. The credit card was never cut up and I maxed it out every time I was fiending/lusting. I knew what I was doing was wrong. Before I had sex, I would always say, "This is the last time"—and, sis, it was NEVER the last time. If you are in the same place I was, know that God isn't pleased and stop convincing yourself that having sex isn't worse than any other sin.

Right your wrongs and show God that you are committed to His kingdom and that you want to do His will. Continue praying and staying faithful. The devil will try to sneak up on us, but we can't let him win. Keep your eyes on God.

EXTERNAL STIMULI

Scientifically speaking, the ability of an organism or organ to respond to external stimuli is called sensitivity. So no matter how sensitive or strong you believe your mind is, external stimuli can and will have an effect on your walk with Christ.

The enemy uses things like social media, television shows, music and even words from various people in our lives, to distract us from the will of God. Think about how many times we correlate music, for instance, with things of our past. Music is probably the easiest way for the enemy to get into our minds and distract us. Think about the lyrics to the music you listen to. Is it really reflective of who God wants you to be? Is it how you even want to portray yourself? How about the different things we see on social media—the gossip, the portrayal of "Hollywood" celebrities' lifestyles that we sit around and watch, desiring to live like them?

Not all external stimuli are used to distract us; in fact, there are several things that we can allow into our lives that have a positive impact. Whether it's hearing the Word of God being preached, consuming healthier foods, reading (or writing) books, and so on, all of these can aid us in becoming healthier individuals in Christ. Positive stimuli or triggers can get you back on track if you are feeling weak or have become mundane in your journey. Doing the right thing is always viewed as harder, but it is often much more rewarding than the things of the world. It is all about what things we allow in and those we seek to avoid in the first place.

DAY 15

DAY 15

Stephan:

In my eyes, teachers are not appreciated nearly as much as they should be. They hold so much weight as potential mentors and examples for our youth.

I have always desired to reach back to the youth to encourage them and make a lasting impact on their lives. Several of my childhood friends work in the school system. It pleases me when I can take part in coaching or speaking to their group of kids because I know I am helping shape someone's future and I don't take it lightly.

I am really considering signing up to be a mentor at church. I am very big on brotherhood and character building. Alexis and I have been discussing joining a ministry at church and committing to helping build within our church community. I haven't made my mind up as far as what ministry I want to join because my work schedule doesn't allow me to be at church and Bible study every Wednesday and Sunday. But the mentorship program allows me to serve and set up a flexible schedule that best fits my mentee and me. When my colleague told me about the mentoring program at church, I was very intrigued due to my passion for youth.

DAY 15

Alexis:

I praised God today, thanking Him for His grace. I couldn't imagine where I would be without it.

Somehow, my undeserving, disobedient, promise-breaking, trifling self is still qualified to be saved by His grace. I repeatedly told God that I was sorry for having sex but I continuously went back on my word. After having unprotected sex and getting my period late, I'd pray and ask God for a negative pregnancy test. Each time I vowed never to have sex again. *Talk about being locked in a pattern of sin.*

I couldn't stop; it was a routine. I found myself doing the same thing over and over again.

I was so scared to be a single mother, but I wasn't scared to disobey God. I lived a double life.

I was an intentional sinner, but I claimed to be saved. I exclaimed how much I loved the Lord but couldn't keep His commandments. I knowingly sinned because I was told that His grace would never run out; I'd just charged it to the game.

I was something else! I will never forget those times. Reflecting on my past reminds me of how good God is.

DAY 16

DAY 16

Stephan:

Our bodies do not belong to us; we are not our own (1 Corinthians 6:19). We have to take care of our gifts; we have to show that we appreciate the temple that God left us with. That includes eating healthy, working out and not fornicating.

Set up a workout schedule and meet your partner at the gym or on the track. Alexis and I love working out together and pushing one another toward our body goals.

DAY 16

Alexis:

I yearn to be so connected with God that I don't look to anyone else for guidance or advice unless He has led me to speak to that person. I want to recognize His voice instantly and not second-guess when He is calling me.

Today I am thankful that He has called one of His sons to travel with me on this journey, running after Him so that we can love each other the right way. I am thankful to know God and have the desire to make such a life-changing decision with the man I love.

I am thankful that we are not locked in a pattern of shameless sin. We all know that if we have cherished sin in our hearts, the Lord will not listen (Psalm 66:18). For God knows our hearts and our true intentions—those we cannot hide, especially not from Him.

DAY 17

DAY 17

Stephan:

Serving within my community always fills my heart with joy. Our neighbors aren't always as blessed as we are. Everyone isn't privileged enough to have clothes on their backs, shoes on their feet or a roof over their heads. It's unfortunate, but it's the world we live in. Get with your loved one and pay the acts of kindness forward. Find a way to pour into your community together.

We are currently birthing a nonprofit organization to improve patient outcomes by helping to make medications more affordable to those who may struggle to keep up with medical expenses.

1 PETER 4:10 As every man hath received the gift, even so minister the same one to another, as good stewards of the manifold grace of God.

DAY 17

Alexis:

Praying, seeking God's voice and fleeing from sin requires a great deal of discipline. And if we don't do those things and adhere to God's word, we will find ourselves further and further away from our purpose.

Closing our legs is only half the battle. As a Christian, it is important to reflect our Lord and Savior and lead by example. Whatever it is that may be holding you hostage is clearly not a good example of our God. Drop it. Ask your boyfriend, accountability partner or pastor to pray with you, not only for deliverance but also for a mind change.

After one long week without sex, go on a date with your significant other and invite Jesus. Make sure He has a seat at the table. Reflect on your journey thus far. Ask your man what his struggles were throughout the week. We need to know what our partners are struggling with. Communicating what our problem areas are, gives us the opportunity to pray and petition God on our partner's behalf.

Women, we will one day be the "keeper of the home." When times get tough, we need to be in a position to pray and bring out our blessed oil. It's important to encourage our future husbands to stay strong and continue to pray for them. (Add a few extra minutes to your normal prayer time just for him. He needs you.)

DAY 18

DAY 18

Stephan:

There is so much power in true friendship. The people you talk to and spend the most time with have a huge influence on your life. We like to think that we make our own choices and don't fall under the category of being peer pressured, but often we do—unintentionally, of course. Sometimes we naturally participate in activities that we wouldn't normally do without our friends. That's why it's important to be surrounded by like-minded individuals with common morals, values and goals.

In this season, it is imperative to have accountability partners. As Christians, we need support and comfort. We need to be prayed for, prayed with and corrected when we are wrong.

It may be difficult to open up and share your personal business, especially concerning your love life, but finding someone trustworthy with good intentions will be beneficial in the long run. Talking about struggles, temptation and life changes with your accountability partner will encourage you to stay on the right path (1 Thessalonians 5:11).

DAY 18

Alexis:

Favor comes when we aren't trying to do what the world is doing. I don't even know where to begin or how to explain what God has done in my life since I've reached this level of obedience.

Sex was my sin that I didn't want to let go of. God knows how stubborn I was when someone told me that I was wrong. I really didn't see the reason behind being celibate, especially because my boyfriend and I had already had sex. It didn't make sense to me and I wasn't trying to make any sense of it.

Sometimes we don't like to acknowledge that hell is real. But the truth is that hell is the final destination for souls who have lived lives of shameless sin. *Shameless sin* is anytime we willfully sin, choosing to disobey the laws of God that we are fully aware of.. We hope that our ultimate and eternal destiny is heaven, but we have to use our time on Earth wisely and according to our hope.

We can't reject God and His truths and then expect to be in His right hand, counted as His sheep and separate from the goats in His left (Matthew 25:31–43). We all like to shout that we are a work in progress during the time of chastisement, and that is fine, as long as we're genuinely working to be more like the God we claim to love.

DAY 19

DAY 19

Stephan:

T he best release is praise and worship. There is nothing greater than worshiping God and showing Him how thankful we are for His grace and mercy.

Today we take time to worship our Lord and Savior for all that He has done for us individually and collectively. We are lifting Him high for ALL things seen and unseen, the haves and the have-nots, the future and the past. God is worthy to be praised on every occasion because, at the end of the day, He is making sure that it will all come together for our good (Romans 8:28).

DAY 19

Alexis:

"You can't diet out fornication; you have to have a mind change!"

-Exclaimed my Pastor during church service.

Those words stuck with me long after service. I thanked the Holy Spirit for delivering that message because I needed to hear what departed from his lips.

Through my many failed attempts of celibacy, I was praying, fasting and crying out to God, but my mind wasn't right. I wasn't having sex because I felt like God didn't want me to. I was performing as if I were trying to change for Jesus—as if I had nothing to gain and I was losing it all. *As if I was doing Him some type of favor.* Who did I think I was? I'm glad I got a reality check and I'm so glad those words departed from my pastor's lips.

I needed a mindset shift. My mind has to continue to serve the Lord. I can't make any deals with Satan by departing from God's laws. The devil offers things that while enticing, result in a lifetime of terrible outcomes.

Allowing your mind to bargain with the devil will have you living in a series of unfortunate events. Been there, done that and I'm not going back. I am walking in my purpose and praying for the strength to fight through every battle that tries to steer me away from King Jesus.

DAY 20

DAY 20

Stephan:

Surrendering our desires to the Lord is one of the most powerful things we can do because, *in our own strength*, we can't make our dreams come to fruition. God has to do it or we may unintentionally force our purpose and end up living outside of His will.

Documenting your feelings, concerns or expectations will allow you to understand them more clearly. Writing your feelings down will give you the opportunity to look back and acknowledge how much you've grown. Alexis and I believe that this tactic gives us the opportunity to control our emotions and improve our mental and spiritual health.

If you haven't already, download a journal app or grab a nice journal from the bookstore and write a little each day!

DAY 20

Alexis:

> **1 CORINTHIANS 7:34** There is a difference *also* between a wife and a virgin. The unmarried woman careth for the things of the Lord, that she may be holy both in body and in spirit: but she that is married careth for the things of the world, how she may please *her* husband.

While we are single, we should cling to God and tune in to him 100%. Sometimes we can get so caught up in planning date nights, bae-cations, birthdays and preparing for the next best thing with our man that we forget about our heavenly Father. In this season, we have to sacrifice our time and make sure we are giving Him the attention He needs. Remember, sis, He is a jealous God.

It's okay to get excited about your future husband. I definitely go above and beyond to plan fun events and appropriate dates with Stephan. But, tonight, I had to check myself.

I spend more time with Stephan than I do with the One that has given me life, grace and forgiveness. I've neglected the One who loves me unconditionally through my messiness and trifling ways. Could you imagine bending over backward for your best friend and then not hearing from her or him for months?

Picture giving all of your friends $100.00 and then not hearing from any of them for two weeks. We can't do God like that! He is love. He is the reason we are in love and know how to love. It's imperative that we acknowledge Him in this beautiful season.

Soon, we will have to shift our focus to pleasing our headship and managing our alone time with the Lord. If it's God's will, children will come and there will be household responsibilities along with work and maybe school. It won't be as difficult if we prepare and form good habits now.

Love your man, attend to your relationship, but do not make the mistake of throwing Jesus by the wayside because you're too wrapped up in the man He blessed you with.

DAY 21

DAY 21

Stephan:

During this time, we must keep the lines of communication open with God. Prayer has to become a lifestyle. Building a relationship with God undergoes the same process you use to build a connection with anyone else. He needs to hear from you, and in order for us to hear from Him, we have to spend time with Him. We need to invite God to travel with us throughout the day and talk to Him regularly. We should converse with God more than anyone else.

Talking to Him doesn't mean that you have to walk around talking to yourself audibly, although sometimes that is what it takes. Try bonding with him spiritually and everything else will come naturally.

Praying gives us an opportunity to intercede for one another. Going before the Most High on behalf of your neighbor is so powerful.

1 TIMOTHY 2:1 I exhort therefore, that, first of all, supplications, prayers, intercessions, and giving of thanks, be made for all men.

DAY 21

Alexis:

I woke up this morning and completely shifted my focus to God. I needed Him to hold my hand today and guide me. My spirit desired for Him to be close.

Have you ever opened your eyes and just felt weary, perhaps a little discouraged? I rebuked those spirits and called on Jesus—I wanted Him to know that I was inviting Him on this journey with me. I wanted Him to hear my cry and urgency for change. We need God on board with our celibacy journey just as much as we want one another. Without him, there would be no progress.

> **ROMANS 13:14** But put ye on the Lord Jesus Christ, and make not provision for the flesh, to fulfil the lusts thereof.

I read this scripture and studied it thoroughly. Imitating Jesus puts us in a position to be meek, pure, chaste and peaceful. His example is the blueprint of how to live a good life. I cried out to God, asking Him to remove me from any situation or person that triggers or excites me to feed my flesh.

My prayer today:

Oh God, I thank You for a mind and heart free of licentious indulgence. Thank You for giving me the desire to chase after You and to labor and make provision for all the real needs of life. God, please make my heart pure and devote my mind to kingdom principles and use me to be a light in the world as a reflection of Your word.

MISSING OUT

It seems like all the saved people in the world are older, deeply rooted in the Word and boring. Doesn't it seem like the majority of saved folk are at least over 30, with nothing else to do but praise God? They're usually real sanctified and souled out, huh? Looks like they came out of the womb as saints. *How in the world can I get on that level, please God and still have fun?* Is what we ask ourselves as we look at them with admiration.

Many of us think it's impossible.

We say that we will put more effort toward being Christ-like once we reach a specific age or milestone in life. We think that we have time and we act like our days are promised, though the Bible has already told us that our days are numbered (Job 14:5–7).

Let's not put so much focus on pleasing our friends and trying to have fun that we conform to this world and forget about our true purpose on Earth. God did not put us here to be miserable. He didn't intend for us to arrive and hate life, but He doesn't want us to take life for granted.

Brothers and sisters, we are here on an assignment. We do not have an infinite amount of time here. It is written in the text, plain as day, that He is coming back. We have to be ready (Matthew 24:43–44).

Challenge yourself to go against the grain. Stand out among the careless sinners and hypocrites. You don't have to change your entire life in one instant and mirror the saints at church, but ask God to change your heart if you're in love with anything that doesn't please Him. Let's not be afraid of missing out in this season because isolating yourself from things and people that will tempt you is best for your soul.

This is the time when we have to call out to God and ask Him to protect us from covetousness and let us desire only the works of His kingdom (Luke 12:15).

Let's continue letting the real author of life order our steps and guard our hearts so that we don't feel like we are letting life pass us by. Being young and saved isn't farfetched and God has placed people here to lighten the journey. Instead of being concerned about missing out, we need to remember that He will make it so that we turn our backs on sin and focus on what lies ahead. He tells us to press toward the prize of the upward call of God in Christ Jesus (Philippians 3:13–14).

DAY 22

DAY 22

Stephan:

I've always been content with stepping away from the crowd when I know the environment isn't in alignment with my spiritual growth. I don't do all the things that I used to do because I've grown.

Club-hopping every weekend and *turning up* at house parties isn't on my weekly to-do list. Short of homecoming and celebrations with my friends, I prefer to go on dates with Alexis or play cards and just hang out with the guys. Everyone has to identify his or her convictions and do what God is telling him or her to do.

God does not desire for us to yield to sin. Always seek Him and ask for His guidance. Sometimes we can plan to go out and have a good time, even at a restaurant or cookout and God will instruct us to stay home. At that point, we have to be obedient and trust the Holy Spirit. God might be protecting us from dangers unseen or something that may be a hindrance to our walk in Christ. Obey Him.

DAY 22

Alexis:

"Missing out" was never a fear of mine until I got to college. My best friend in high school was saved and my other friends had strict parents, so even if we did talk about boys, sex and parties, our parents did not know about it. I did not have to worry about feeling out of place because we all had similar household rules. But college was a different story.

People spoke freely about casual sex and getting drunk and few were intentional about their spiritual growth. Going to church on Sunday was optional and Bible study was out of the question for many students. At one point, I didn't know if I was selling myself short and turning my back on everything that college was supposed to be about or if I was doing the right thing. I never enjoyed going to the club or getting drunk and I definitely was not interested in sleeping around, but there was a time when I questioned myself and said, "Is that what you should be doing?"

Although I wouldn't say I was a dedicated Christian at that point in my life, I knew that I was stronger in my walk than most of the people I hung around. Often they'd laugh and say that I didn't do anything or go anywhere, but that didn't bother me because I didn't share the same interests. In times like these, when you feel as though you are missing out, pray and seek wise counsel.

Speak to someone who has been where you are and also try to find friends who have the same goals as you. It didn't take long for me to shake my fear, but it haunted me for a few weeks. That was a short but very depressing stage in my life.

DAY 23

DAY 23

We absolutely love fellowshipping with our friends and discussing life, school, goals and God. It's always interesting to share your triumphs as well as trials and tribulations with your loved ones. We have an amazing group of friends and most of them are in relationships.

Fortunately, the majority of us are on our way toward getting engaged or married. It's truly a blessing to have such an amazing group of people to love and live with.

During this season of being rooted in the Word, we must engage with believers of Christ Jesus. Try to hang out in groups of people who have similar goals and aspirations. It can be difficult surrounding yourself with people who don't understand your relationship or your love for the Lord.

> *Dear God, we come to you today, humbly kneeling to the Most High, asking for your guidance and the beautiful gift of friendship. Send us friends who can help us through our hardships and support us through the draining seasons. We want the joy, encouragement and trust that comes with good friendship. We want loved ones who share their lives, not just the gospel.*
>
> *We praise You in advance for friends who bring wisdom and positivity, right now, in the name of Jesus. Thank You, Lord, for bringing us company that loves You above everything else. In Your most gracious and glorious name, we pray and say Amen.*

DAY 24

DAY 24

Stephan:

Vacationing is how I reward myself after long weeks of hard work. I really enjoy getting up with the guys and catching up on life. A few of my buddies and I go on at least one international trip a year and I always look forward to that.

It is a blessing to be able to see so many different cultures and ways of living across the world. Alexis and I also use vacations as a way to step out of our normal routine and see all that our travels have to offer.

Vacationing while being celibate is very different from when we were having sex. However, we are still blessed to be able to travel rather than stay stagnant and afraid to do the things we have always loved to do. I believe that you and your loved one should do your best to reward one another with a trip or do the things you have always enjoyed if you can without breaking your promise to God.

Alexis and I have a couple's vacation coming up this summer. The same rules that we've set thus far will remain while we are on our vacation in L.A. Our friends are well aware of our goal and we will still have a good time with the other couples without indulging in sexual activity.

1 PETER 5:8 Be sober, be vigilant; because your adversary the devil, as a roaring lion, walketh about, seeking whom he may devour:

DAY 24

Alexis:

"Bae-cationing" is the highlight of my year! I love it when Stephan and I book a vacation. Although our sex life has been put on hold, I'm still just as excited to hop on a cruise ship or a flight.

I would agree that vacations can be tempting, but a way to eliminate the temptation and "mess-ups" is to travel in a group. Invite your accountability partners or travel with couples who support your celibacy journey.

Keep close to you the people who want to see you succeed at waiting to have sex until marriage. Let them correct you and check you if you need to be checked.

> **PROVERBS 27:17** Iron sharpeneth iron;
> so a man sharpeneth the countenance
> of his friend.

DAY 25

DAY 25

Stephan:

T alking about the future excites us. I know that God has great plans for His children and we cannot wait to continue to grow in Him. Not only do I want to receive all the blessings that God has for me, but also be in a position to bless others freely.

Finances are a huge factor in our success and life goals. It is important that we practice wise spending now, including paying tithes and offerings. We have to submit to biblical exhortations by doing our best to commit to all that our heavenly Father has asked us to do.

Being tightfisted during the time of tithes and offerings won't bless us. Saving our money and tithing will only put us in a position to be blessed abundantly (Luke 6:38).

DAY 25

Alexis:

Although our main focus in this season is abstaining from sex until marriage, I enjoy working on other areas in my life that need improvement. I love to shop, eat out and decorate. Often I have to remind myself that I am still in college and I can't spend money like it grows on trees. Sometimes I find myself in furniture stores for hours, knowing that I don't have any business trying to buy a new couch.

I'd like to think that I am doing better, though. For the past year and a half, I've used the Digit app, which has helped me save so much money! Digit makes saving withdrawals directly from my checking account almost daily and I never miss the money. I don't see it, I don't touch it and I don't spend it!

Remember that the Bible instructs us to save money and states that it is a wise practice for various reasons.

> **PROVERBS 22:7** The rich ruleth over the poor, and the borrower is servant to the lender.

DAY 26

DAY 26

Stephan:

As we grow older and wiser, we begin separating from childish ways. Sometimes that includes friends.

Walking with God may require us to leave some relationships behind and we have to be ready to do that.

I always try to remember that obedience is better than sacrifice. If God is telling you to separate from long-lasting friendships, try to make that change immediately.

Thankfully, all of my friends are believers, but some of us are more committed than others. That doesn't mean that we can't "kick it" or that we have to stop being friends. I enjoy sharing what God is doing in my life and encouraging them to continue growing in Christ, as many brothers and sisters have encouraged me.

Now isn't the time to part from everyone who isn't as dedicated as you are (unless the Lord tells you to do so), but be a light to the world and encourage your friends to live for Jesus.

> **PROVERBS 18:24** A man that hath friends must shew himself friendly: and there is a friend that sticketh closer than a brother.

DAY 26

Alexis:

> **1 CORINTHIANS 15:33** Be not deceived: evil communications corrupt good manners.

I love this scripture and I find it to be true. I don't know about you, but I have found myself in unfortunate situations because I was hanging with the wrong crowd. During that time, I wasn't wise enough to stand up for what was right. Everything my mother taught me went out the window and I found myself engaging in conversations that I knew I shouldn't have been part of and behaving like I was raised by a two-year-old.

I remember exactly where I was when I said my first curse word. Every time I read this scripture (1 Corinthians 15:33), God easily focuses my attention on that day. I was very young and didn't know anything about cursing, let alone cursing anyone out. But because I was with my older cousins who cursed freely when adults weren't around, I began mimicking them. Before I knew it, I was cursing like a sailor.

Since my renewed love for Christ, I've always reflected on that day and it means so much. I can't sit back and do what everyone else is doing. If I can't speak up and tell my friends what's right, then I can't hang with them. Regardless of what the topic is, I should be able to state biblical facts that support my opinion and not be made fun of or laughed at.

You'd think that people wouldn't taunt those who love the Lord, but it still happens. Good friends wouldn't encourage you to do anything against your morals and values. We have to do our best to flee from those who encourage us to backslide. We don't have to dislike them, but it would be in our best interest to continue praying for them while loving them from a distance.

DAY 27

DAY 27

Tonight we came together and discussed things that we should give less of our time to like certain television shows and social media. We realized that it could be a distraction for us as we move forward with intense Bible study and professional development.

We know that times may be getting tough and it seems like we have to separate ourselves from everything and everyone. At this point, you may feel like you're missing out on life because you're a Christian, not just because you're celibate. You might feel it most when you're sitting at a table with folk claiming to be saved while willfully indulging in sinful activities without caution or fear. These same folk look at you like you're crazy when you can't relate or laugh at you because of your sudden change and commitment. It might get tough, but you must fight the fear of missing out and being ridiculed. Remember, they talked about Jesus too.

We have to continue standing out and standing up for Jesus as He stood for us! We can't be part of everything; the fear of missing out will distract us from Christ and take our eye off the bigger picture. Comparing our lives to our friends' lives is unnecessary because God will bless us for *our* obedience. He knows our struggle and He recognizes the difficulty in fighting our flesh, especially in the early stages of making life-changing decisions.

We like to think of our spiritual journey as a process in which we yield to God and move when He tells us to. We are a work in progress. We didn't make this transition overnight; we didn't do a 180-degree turn all at once. We are simply looking forward, praying and asking God for direction as we focus on doing what is right. Continue being righteous because the Holy Spirit is upon you and He will see you through.

THE POWER OF PRAYER

God's word has commanded us to pray. Ephesians 6:18 tells us to pray in the Spirit on all occasions with all kinds of prayers and requests. Prayer is how we communicate with God.

During this sacred time, we have the opportunity to pour our hearts out, requesting miracles and forgiveness. Like us, you may still be struggling with celibacy. Every day is an uphill battle, whether protecting your thoughts, praying regularly, spending time with God or lusting over your significant other. Praise God that we can overcome these battles by taking our struggles to the Lord. He is always excited to hear from us; He wants a relationship with His children, which can only grow through communication.

God is pleased with us—He is proud of our growing prayer life and commitment to His kingdom. The living God acknowledges the struggles that come with withdrawing ourselves from evil. Obstacles that appear to be impossible to overcome on this journey are nothing in God's eyes. He can make our journey lighter by moving people and things out of the way that were meant to distract us. We must realize that some things can only be handled in the spiritual realm. In some instances, all we can do is call upon God to grant us power over evil.

DAY 28

Dear Heavenly Father,

We come to You today asking that You forgive us for our sins. We are asking that you make our hearts and thoughts pure, oh God. We abandon ourselves to You, Lord. We give our souls to You with infinite trust.

Thank You in advance for another successful day free of fornication. God, we love You and praise You for granting us another opportunity to get it right.

Amen.

LEVITICUS 18:20 Moreover thou shalt not lie carnally with thy neighbour's wife, to defile thyself with her.

DAY 29

Father, we need You. You are our rock and our salvation.

With You, God, we know that we cannot be moved. We rebuke every stronghold over our relationship in the name of Jesus.

God, keep us grounded and true to our faith. Remove every distraction; release us from people and things that are not of You.

We acknowledge that You have called us to a celibate lifestyle. In this season of being true to the calling, we ask that You make it easy for us to turn our backs on our wicked ways. We seek holiness in the body and the spirit and pray for Your everlasting grace and favor over our lives.

Protect us and guide us as we travel on this uphill journey; in Your son Jesus's name we pray.

Amen.

MALACHI 3:5 And I will come near to you to judgment; and I will be a swift witness against the sorcerers, and against the adulterers, and against false swearers, and against those that oppress the hireling in his wages, the widow, and the fatherless, and that turn aside the stranger from his right, and fear not me, saith the LORD of hosts.

DAY 30

Dear God,

We come to You humbly, asking that You keep us during the trying times.

Keep us free of masturbation, for we know it leads to bondage. Your word says that suffering produces perseverance, character and hope. We yield to You, knowing that You will reward us with good fruit due to our obedience. Please continue to redirect our thoughts as our minds begin to wander. Keep us from temptation as we move forward.

We trust the process, Lord, and we glorify You for all things seen and unseen. Thank You, God, for giving us another chance to become better individuals. We appreciate You trusting us with this gift and allowing us to share our testimony with Your children.

Amen.

PROVERBS 6:32 But whoso committeth adultery with a woman lacketh understanding: he that doeth it destroyeth his own soul.

DAY 31

Dear God,

We come to You today, asking You to guard our hearts. Continue making us over to who You have called us to be. God, we are praying for patience in this waiting process. We cast out all the spirits of perversion and lust, in the name of Jesus.

We receive the spirit of Holiness in our lives to walk in sexual purity. Help us lay down our tangled thoughts and restive emotions.

As we wait on You, we will stand on Your word in order to give us peace and direction. We thank You for Your refreshing word and unwavering favor.

In your son Jesus's name, Amen.

JEREMIAH 13:27 I have seen thine adulteries, and thy neighings, the lewdness of thy whoredom, and thine abominations on the hills in the fields. Woe unto thee, O Jerusalem! wilt thou not be made clean? when shall it once be?

DAY 32

Father God,

We come to You today, praying against temptation. Behold us, oh Lord, at Your feet! Keep us from falling into the same sin that we successfully ran from. Let us recourse to You when we are tempted. Let us not go backward, dishonoring You, Father God.

You are our strength, and we can do all things through You, who will free our hearts from sinful thoughts. We acknowledge that You have all power in your hands, God. We know that You can fix it to where we do not desire to participate in anything that is not of You. We ask that You loose the chains that bind us and allow us to rise above all the troubles in this world.

Amen.

1 CORINTHIANS 6:9-10 9 Know ye not that the unrighteous shall not inherit the kingdom of God? Be not deceived: neither fornicators, nor idolaters, nor adulterers, nor effeminate, nor abusers of themselves with mankind,

10 Nor thieves, nor covetous, nor drunkards, nor revilers, nor extortioners, shall inherit the kingdom of God.

DAY 33

Dear God,

We thank You for another day above ground. We thank You for allowing us to have one another and be on this journey together. We thank You for pushing us to grow stronger and wiser in Christ.

As we continue loving and learning one another, we ask that You help us discern Your will. We want to walk in Your ways and be sensitive to the prodding of Your spirit. We want to hear Your voice, oh God, and recognize Your signs; make it plain for us, oh God.

We desire to one day have a ministry that blesses You, Father God. We want to win souls. Please position us so that we can be used and work diligently for Your kingdom.

You've redeemed us from the past and forgiven us for our wicked ways, and we thank You every day for Your love and grace.

Amen.

1 CORINTHIANS 6:18 Flee from sexual immorality. All other sins a person commits are outside the body, but whoever sins sexually, sins against their own body.

DAY 34

Dear Heavenly Father,

Fill us with love, joy, faith and wisdom. We thank You for the happiness and patience that You've given us. We seek Your blessing, hoping that You will allow us to spend the rest of our lives together if it's Your will.

If You see fit, God, we ask for healthy children and grandchildren. We ask that You continue filling our hearts with love for one another. Help us keep the trust and respect for one another over the many years to come. Help us communicate and listen diligently. Allow us to be debt-free, God, lenders and not borrowers.

May you continue to protect and guide us as we travel the dangerous highways. Please continue keeping our thoughts pure as we yield to You and walk in our calling.

Thank You, God, for hearing our prayer.

Amen.

> **REVELATION 2:22** Behold, I will cast her into a bed, and them that commit adultery with her into great tribulation, except they repent of their deeds.

LOVE

Of all the choices we can make in life, who we choose to marry is by far the most important. An unhealthy marriage can change the course of our entire lives. Practicing and facing the many changes during celibacy will allow us to experience a different level of commitment and dedication before tying the knot.

Choosing who we wish to love and experience life with is very exciting. The butterflies are forever flying in our stomachs and our cheeks hurt from smiling in admiration of our significant other. Although those moments never get old and the fun times go too soon, we have to find a way to go beneath the joyful moments and discuss uncomfortable topics so that we know that we will always love our future spouse (even if there are times when we don't like him or her).

We don't get to select our family members and, sometimes as children, are forced to be friends with people that we could've lived without. Considering those things, we should embrace this season of learning our partners so when the going gets tough and frustration arises, we know who we are dealing with. We won't fight fire with fire but choose love over hate, knowing our partner versus a façade often presented in the heat of the moment.

Love isn't always pretty; it comes with a price. With God on our side, we know that sometimes we have to lose a few battles to win the war. That is love.

DAY 35

DAY 35

Stephan:

I believe a part of love is praying for one another. There is no greater way to communicate that you love someone than with prayer.

I've been praying for God to strengthen Alexis as she takes on another semester of pharmacy school. I really want to see her do well and walk in her calling. I've always admired how giving she is and her willingness to help others. She makes me so proud to be her man. I thank God regularly for such a beautiful soul.

Alexis is an amazing friend, beyond everything else, and I truly appreciate her. It's so easy to fall in love with her and I can see her love for me through our many talks and her unlimited kind gestures. Almost every day serves as a confirmation that God created her for me.

This week, Alexis and I are really connecting on a personal level and spending extra quality time together. We are taking a step back from the weekly dates out on the town and making sure that we get that one-on-one time. Outside of eating dinner together and watching our favorite television series, we call each other on our breaks instead of texting. When we talk, we talk about personal and professional growth and pray for one another in specific areas of need.

Please remember that being in love and preparing for marriage is selfless. As the man and the future head of the house, I have to practice putting myself aside and choosing to act with the love of Christ now. As we've all heard before, we have a long journey ahead of us and choosing love is always the right way to go.

DAY 35

Alexis:

These days, we see so many people divorcing and walking away from their families without a care in the world. That honestly breaks my heart.

Unlike Stephan, I come from a broken home so, needless to say, I don't have a great example of marriage in my life and I am learning as I go. God knows that I want a long-lasting marriage with Stephan; I tell Him this all the time.

People always ask me, as I am sure they probably ask you, "Well, when is the wedding?" At one point it pissed me off because, in my opinion, it is a personal question. What if Stephan didn't want to marry me? Some things people just shouldn't ask, but as we can't control what others do, I had to make some changes on my own.

I had to realize that just because Stephan and I are in love doesn't mean we are ready for marriage. I reminded myself that marriage is a ministry that I am not quite ready to take on—especially since we were having sex every chance we got. But thank God, I can look back on those times and realize that I was wrong. Praise God that we stood through the test of time and didn't let Satan take us under.

DAY 36

DAY 36

Stephan:

I don't know if 36 days is something to celebrate for you, but I am rejoicing! A year ago we were talking the talk but not walking the walk. I said what I could do but never did it.

This is a great feeling. Not only am I proud of Alexis and myself, but I know this is also pleasing to God. Loving Alexis God's way is strengthening our relationship with one another and Christ. I've always considered our relationship healthy, but since acknowledging that sex before marriage is unauthorized, it has reached another level.

Working out, eating healthier, fasting, prayer and everything else that we've decided to focus on, has helped us tremendously. The devil thought that he had us beat by making it seem like all was well when we were sinning. We are raining on his parade by making it through yet another day without falling into one of his traps.

Simply ask God to keep you during the moments when you feel like you want to give up. Some days will be tougher than others, but as long as you keep the line of communication open with God, you will make it.

DAY 36

Alexis:

I remember talking to one of my sisters in Christ, and she said:

"I love God so much that I can't bring myself to have sex!"

When those words left her lips, my heart melted. I was at a loss for words and in deep admiration of how much she loved God. Those words never left me. At this very moment, I smile while reminiscing on that conversation we shared. I wasn't practicing celibacy at that time. We tried but failed miserably. We didn't love Christ like we said we did. We were cheating and betraying Him by taking advantage of His grace, not even thinking about how our actions were hurting Him.

I'm not sure if my friend knows that her expression changed my stance as a Christian woman. I don't even know that she knew my struggle with trying to become celibate, but she made a difference.

I encourage you to share your love for Christ with your friends, classmates, co-workers and everyone in between, because your story may change someone's life. My sister's words have stuck with me over the years and stand as a true testament of why I am where I am today.

DAY 37

DAY 37

Stephan:

As a man, temptation is real therefore everything we do has to be calculated. We even have to flirt gracefully because one thing easily leads to another. Alexis and I have a history of going from 0 to 100 quick.

We have boundaries that we don't even need to discuss. On Valentine's Day, we don't need to listen to slow jams or watch movies in bed because we know exactly where that's going to lead us. Making out isn't something we do often because we know we will be back at square one faster than we can blink.

We continued to experience drawbacks toward the beginning of our journey because we kept entering the red-zone. We pushed buttons that we knew were off limits and continued to do so. It eventually became a pattern. Once a month is just as bad as having sex every day.

You've made the decision and your actions should align with that. Obedience has its bonuses.

DAY 37

Alexis:

I am so thankful that God gave us another opportunity to get it right. Not only have we been granted the opportunity to love one another on a different level, but our obedience also led us to our new ministry.

While helping ourselves, God has given us the opportunity to help others. I have peace during this process of waiting because I know that God is working. In due time it will all come together and work for our good.

Today I had to ask God to break my heart for things that are not like Him. Sometimes I find myself thinking about sex and daydreaming about things that shouldn't be on my mind. I had to say to myself, "Lex, stop dancing with the devil. Don't even give him the satisfaction; you are better than this." Being celibate physically but lusting is not okay.

I had to be real with myself and say, "*God created sex and everything else under the sun. When He is ready for you to get married and experience those things with your husband, then those intense thoughts are okay. But right now, keep your eyes on Him and pray long and hard when your mind wanders where it shouldn't be!*"

I am thankful for this experience. I know that it will strengthen our relationship and reduce the chances of infidelity during our marriage. I definitely don't want disobedience to resurface and catch us. This is the time for us to focus and intentionally work to expel sinful spirits that cause us to be disobedient. I/we don't need anything that will push us away from our heavenly Father.

DAY 38

DAY 38

Stephan:

Taking sex off the table allowed me to enjoy the innocent acts of being in a relationship. Hugs, conversations and quality time mean so much more than they used to. I wouldn't say that I used to take those moments for granted, but I didn't realize how meaningful they were.

Celibacy pushes you to express your love in ways that are pleasing to God and respectful to your partner. I love surprising Alexis with her favorite takeout, flowers, cards and sweet messages. The past few years have been great with her and I am doing my best to continue keeping a smile on her face. She is my blessing and I appreciate her pushing me to do better and loving me enough to keep me lifted in prayer.

DAY 38

Alexis:

Today my spirit was led to pray for Stephan's focus and discipline. I've prayed for him briefly over the past few days but not as much as I've prayed for myself (as if I were on this journey all alone).

I was sitting in class, thinking about my career and where it may take me. And of course, when I think about different practices of pharmacy, I instantly think of Stephan. I shot him a text and asked him how his day was going. He told me that the pharmacy was busy and that one of his colleagues was irritating him. I told him that I would say a special prayer for him.

Thank You, oh God, for all of the blessings that you've bestowed upon us. Thank You for blessing us when we are wrong and unworthy of Your everlasting favor and grace.

God, I come to You humbly, yearning to recognize and better hear Your voice. I'm praying that Stephan and I continue to yield to You and Your word. I pray for his strength and energy on his job, his decision making and his focus.

God, let him keep his eyes on You. I bind the spirit of frustration right now and I pray that he will continue to submit to You in every situation and circumstance.

Thank You, Father God, for allowing us to make it through another day of celibacy under Your anointing. God, use us, push us and place us in the path of our purpose.

In Proverbs 16:3, Your word says, "Commit your work to the Lord, and your plans will be established." This is all about You, oh God; we know that You called us to live for You and be a light to the world by being a reflection of Your word. Unlock our brains and continue to use us! In the name of Jesus.

Amen.

DAY 39

DAY 39

Stephan:

I remember when Alexis presented the idea of us journaling and one day turning our journals into a blog, book or a gift to another couple.

This caught me by surprise, as Alexis is an extremely private person. I was actually pretty uncomfortable with the idea myself and I'm usually more open to others than she is.

What bothered me the most was the idea of "preaching" to people about what they should and shouldn't be doing. I didn't feel like it was my place, especially as we didn't have a long track record of being celibate and I don't feel like I am exactly where God wants me to be.

Although I still feel uneasy about preaching to another person, I am thankful that God has us on this assignment because most of the things that I share or discuss aren't concepts that I've mastered. I still battle with a few things but, as I write and reflect, it allows me to document my thoughts and what has helped me get through. Not only can other men out there read and apply it to their lives, but I can also go back and read while continuing to grow.

I can't praise God enough for pulling Alexis and me out of bondage! Our relationship has grown tremendously. The chemistry has not gone anywhere; we love harder and we are closer to our ultimate goal.

DAY 39

Alexis:

I like to think that my relationship is my ministry. I don't mind sharing what God has brought me through with close peers or relatives. For a while, I viewed this as if I was telling my business to people and allowing them to have an ear in on what was going on in my life. But God showed me very quickly that my life is His. My testimony shouldn't be kept between myself and those whom I felt comfortable sharing with. I need to open up and show people what dating God's way has done for me.

Eventually, I began to share the dynamics of my relationship with strangers and classmates. God also spoke to me and said that I needed to love everyone with the love of Christ—not just Stephan, my friends or my family. This meant that I had to go back and mend friendships that didn't end well and apologize to people whom I hurt in the past.

We can't claim that we love Christ but treat our brothers and sisters any kind of way.

So if you've cursed someone out or ended a friendship on a bad note, try to revisit the situation and make it right. You don't necessarily have to rekindle the relationship, but do what you can to iron out the wrinkles. We've all been kept by grace and the Lord forgives us daily, so let's pay it forward by putting out fires and blowing away the smoke.

DAY 40

DAY 40

Stephan:

I love God because of who He is. I appreciate everything that He has guided me to and protected me from! I know I wouldn't be where I am today without a praying family. It was their prayers that kept me through school and out of harm's way. Some plots were designed to trap me but, because of prayer and God's grace, I didn't get caught up. Even when I was wrong, He still made everything right.

After I continued to backslide and fall short, He still blessed me. At this point in life, I am spiritually mature enough to identify the mistakes that I made in the past. The only thing I can do now is repent and do my best to calculate my actions moving forward. No one is perfect and there's always room for growth but, at some point, we shouldn't feel comfortable doing the same things we did before we got saved. Doing the same things over and over and expecting a different result is the true definition of insanity.

Living up to religion isn't easy, but working to please God is. Taking a step back and analyzing the One behind it all excites me and always pushes me to do better. He sacrificed His only son to save you and me. When we think about how much God loves us and what He sacrificed, we should want to level up and try to repay Him by submitting to His word.

As I continue to pray and study the Bible, I try to apply it to my life with great effort. It hasn't always been easy and I haven't always been consistent, but God knows my heart. He knows our intentions. We just have to do our best to be obedient and give reverence to God for all things. The journey is so much lighter when we continue to fall in love with Christ and work every day to be more like Him.

DAY 40

Alexis:

Today the spirit of the Lord is telling me to work on my actions. He is telling me to make sure that my actions are lining up with my decision to be celibate. I know exactly what He's talking about.

I can identify my laziness on this journey. Sometimes I let school and everything else that's going on, take priority over the time that I need to be spending with God. Through my mistakes in the past, I've learned that celibacy will not work if you are not praying or spending a significant amount of time with God.

I've always admired Stephan's prayer life. I am usually anxious and on edge during difficult times, whereas he is usually calm in the presence of a storm because he has already prayed. My faith is always strong because I know what God can do, but I have to top it off with a prayer and ask God for what I need. I always thank Stephan for reminding me to pray when I go to him, crying and frustrated about problems that I haven't professed to God. His response is always the same: "Well, have you prayed about it?" or "I am not the one you need to talk to . . ." while pointing upward and then offering to pray aloud together. Because of his relationship with God, I've never worried about him stepping out on our relationship during this time and, thankfully, he has never tried to pressure me into having sex with him.

At this point, I know that I need to build my relationship with God and not be content with where I am. Abstaining from sex isn't enough. All of my energy doesn't need to go into my celibacy journey. I need to channel some energy toward Christ and toward strengthening my prayer life.

DAY 41

DAY 41

Stephan:

> **1 CORINTHIANS 13:4-8** Charity suffereth long, and is kind; charity envieth not; charity vaunteth not itself, is not puffed up, Doth not behave itself unseemly, seeketh not her own, is not easily provoked, thinketh no evil; Rejoiceth not in iniquity, but rejoiceth in the truth; Beareth all things, believeth all things, hopeth all things, endureth all things. Charity never faileth: but whether there be prophecies, they shall fail; whether there be tongues, they shall cease; whether there be knowledge, it shall vanish away.

That is a powerful scripture. The text tells us that love never fails. Could you imagine where we'd be emotionally if we did everything in life with love or if we committed acts of kindness without expecting anything in return? We have to forgive one another, treat people right and love our neighbors with the love of Jesus Christ.

Fostering a healthy relationship with our significant other and Jesus is good, but it isn't enough. We have to continue praying to God, asking for Godly love so that we can willingly cleanse ourselves from our selfish ways. God wants us to love strangers and enemies, even if they've treated us badly. He wants all of our actions and words to come from love.

People will forget what you said, they'll forget what you did, but they'll never forget how you made them feel. It isn't always easy to do, but acts of love and compassion go a long way.

Hold the door open for someone today or tomorrow if it's too late for today. Showing love doesn't take much effort and it doesn't have to be anything big. Apologize to your cousin whom you fell out with years ago over something petty or bless a friend with a love offering. Why should we hold grudges when God forgives us for our sinful ways?

One of the principles I hold myself to is not holding grudges. These are character-building moments that we need in preparation for our serious relationships, parenthood and life in general.

DAY 41

Alexis:

God is so good. He really never gets tired of blessing His people and making a way out of no way. When I tell you that He has been in the neighborhood delivering blessings left and right, I mean it! I am getting A's on exams that I thought I failed, my friends are graduating as first-generation college students, relationships are being mended and new businesses are popping up left and right. That's just a highlight of what God is doing in this season.

As I watched God work in excitement, He showed me that there is so much more. I thought I knew, but God was trying to tell me that I was going to miss my blessing by being mean and stubborn. For some reason, I thought that I could greet people at the front doors of the church and post inspirational messages on Facebook but have animosity toward old friends. This was a tough pill to swallow.

Tonight, I called my best friend and shared what I thought God was instructing me to do and of course she agreed. I couldn't believe that God really wanted me to call people and apologize for things that I didn't even think I did wrong. I told my friend that I would take my time apologizing because I wasn't ready and she simply asked me how I would feel if God took His time doing things that I asked Him to do.

Once I thought about how God has always been on time, blessing me with what I've asked for and more, I did what needed to be done and I am happy. It feels good not to have bad blood with anyone. I am thanking God for conviction and for pushing me to do what needed to be done.

DAY 42

DAY 42

Today we are focusing on a few Bible scriptures and committing them to memory. We've decided to post them in our cars and reference them in our prayers.

As we continue to make evident changes in our lifestyle, it is our goal to hold one another accountable as we learn about Christ. We made a promise to encourage one another to read the Bible, learn scriptures and apply them to our lives.

> **LUKE 6:35** But love ye your enemies, and do good, and lend, hoping for nothing again; and your reward shall be great, and ye shall be the children of the Highest: for he is kind unto the unthankful and to the evil.

> **ROAMANS 12:9** Let love be without dissimulation. Abhor that which is evil; cleave to that which is good.

> **EPHESIANS 4:2** With all lowliness and meekness, with longsuffering, forbearing one another in love.

ORAL SEX

While practicing celibacy, oral sex is off limits. Giving and receiving oral sex conflicts with the purpose and the practice of celibacy. Just because sexual intercourse isn't happening doesn't mean that it is okay. ALL sexual activity must be prohibited until marriage.

After participating in these activities for years—some for over a decade—it will be hard.

It would be so much easier to put sex on the back burner if you could receive oral sex in its absence. But we aren't trying to fill a void with another sin. We are trying to be more like Christ and to not give in when times get rough.

Pray. *"Cast thy burden upon the LORD, and he shall sustain thee: he shall never suffer the righteous to be moved"* (Psalm 55:22). God literally has our back! We have to keep the line of communication open with Him so that we can recognize His voice and identify His warning.

There will be times when hormones begin to rise and your emotions may try to overtake you, but God will keep you. You'll know when to go home or leave the room. Eventually, we will get to the point where we know the "red zones" but, right now, it's still the beginning. We are learning to love the right way, with the same person. It isn't abnormal to fall into a trap or think that we can handle things that we can't. As we fall and bump our heads, we have to thank God for His sufficient grace and mercy. Bandage up the "boo-boo" and learn from your mistake.

Don't hold yourself hostage if you were too touchy-feely after date night or if you almost went too far. Just pray about it and communicate your weaknesses with Jesus as you reflect on what happened. Ask Him to free you. He already knows that we aren't perfect, so we have to come to terms with the fact that all have sinned and fall short of the glory of God (Romans 3:23).

We've had a tough time in this area. God released us from having sex fast, but we struggled with being caressed, making out and having oral sex. Oral sex doesn't create a baby, but it still clouds judgment and mental intimacy with both your significant other and God. We have to continue feeding our spirits so that they can dominate our fleshly desires.

To reach a higher level of spirituality, we know that we have to read the Bible, be true to ourselves and make sure God is our number one priority. As we continue to experiment and make changes within our relationship, we want to stay grounded in the Word. We know that the Bible is the word of God and that it is true. Please join us as we dig into the scripture, highlighting the importance of abstaining from all sexual immorality before marriage.

DAY 43

DAY 43

Stephan:

As the days pass by, having patience has gotten easier. I've created new routines that keep me grounded and focused on the more important things in life.

I've always known that abstaining from sex was the right thing to do and I know it's going to be worth it. I believe that some of God's greatest work will surface during this season. My relationship with God is stronger and I've been concentrating on personal growth. The best part about it is that I am not attempting to do this alone: God is in my corner! The Holy Spirit is within me and I know it. He has given me hope; my faith has moved fear out of the way and my prayers have been answered. God has given me peace like never before and I am so happy that I made this life-changing commitment.

An extremely precious and valuable commodity for a man to possess is patience. Staying steadfast to your commitments is honorable. This walk will strengthen your self-control, humility and commitment. As we continue moving forward, we will receive personal revelations from God by being living examples of the Word and asking Him to reveal His will to us through the Holy Ghost.

DAY 43

Alexis:

As I learn to recognize the promptings of the spirit and the patterns that God uses to get my attention, I like to take notes. I don't do it all the time, but it's nice to have something to reference during my alone time with the Lord. I take notes on what I learn in church, my personal feelings and even my ideas. My notes app on my iPhone is literally my entire life. If someone got ahold of that, they'd have Alexis Dominique Jones figured out.

Rereading my notes allows me to identify my growth and, believe it or not, my past is what keeps me going. Remembering all the times when I tried to figure life out on my own without giving God reverence, makes me want to wait on His approval before making the simplest move.

It took me a long time to figure out that if the Holy Spirit guides me, I will not fail. My hardheaded, jacked-up self, had to fall on my behind far too many times before I let Jesus take the wheel. But as the old folks would say, "A hard head makes a soft behind" and mine is so soft that I ain't trying to fall on it anymore.

DAY 44

DAY 44

Stephan:

Today I am encouraged and looking forward to growing in my walk with God as I want to complete reading the Bible in a timely manner. What I will be reading from—Alexis will too—is a couples' devotional Bible. Alexis and I really believe that reading this version of the Bible will allow us to enhance our relationship by applying the principles of scripture to our lives.

The Bible includes devotions, which include "Marriage Builders" questions, designed to help us talk about real issues within our own unique relationship. So not only am I excited about getting more knowledge of all the promises God has for me but now I will be able to work on laying a stronger foundation for my potential marriage while reading His word.

DAY 44

Alexis:

God is elevating me from things that I never thought I'd depart from. I know that God is getting ready to blow my mind and take my life in a different direction, but that requires a different level of commitment.

Many of us say we want the *move of God,* but that requires us to cut out things that we often don't want to let go. For me to walk in my calling and survive Canaan, I have to be prepared and the time to prepare is now.

God is telling me that He wants me to speak up about what He is doing in my life. He's telling me to stop keeping all His blessings on the down-low. God spoke these things to me today as I was driving to class. My favorite Plies song came on the radio and everyone who knows me knows that I love Plies. Can you believe that I blasted the music and couldn't even bring myself to say the words?

It was an out-of-body experience. I was disgusted with the words and completely turned off. I knew it was God. How in the world can I share a post on social media about celibacy and meet one of my Instagram followers at the red light blasting "Get You Wet"? That's just not right. God is saying that it is time to put provocative music to rest and feed my spirit with good fruit.

Don't just talk about it, practice what you preach.

DAY 45

DAY 45

Stephan:

Today Alexis asked me what my favorite scripture was. It didn't take me long to answer that one:

> **PROVERBS 22:6** Train up a child in the way he should go, and when he is old he will not depart from it.

I love this one because I know this to be true. I am a walking testimony of this scripture!

My parents, grandparents and everyone else in my village, directed me to the Lord and this word never left me. I received wisdom through discipline and I thank my parents for it because I am reaping the benefits of the seeds they sowed.

The teaching of topics like forgiveness is such an important lesson because we all need to position ourselves to repent when we've sinned. We must remain in a repentant state. It doesn't matter if you've been strung out on crack cocaine for years—stealing, killing or worse. All you have to do is ask God for forgiveness and you're forgiven. Period. God's love for us will never fade.

Unfortunately, everyone wasn't taught about God's grace. All of us weren't blessed with parents who knew the word of God well enough to instill it in us. That's why we have to spread the gospel, assuring our peers that our past can't block the blessings to come or God's favor for our future.

DAY 45

Alexis:

W e serve a living God. His presence is within us, His hand is in our lives and His word is not a lie. As the devil arises during this time of change, we have to shut him down. He wants to sneak up on us and make us feel like we aren't growing. The devil wants to stop us because we have millions of people connected to the fruit of our obedience. We can't let Satan block our blessing by confusing us into opting out of our assignment. *Remember what happened to Adam and Eve.*

The devil uses simple things that we don't identify as a big deal to deter us from our task. I almost called into work because the spirit of sleepiness fell over me. Praise God that I rebuked it and continued on my way! Can you believe that if I had been late today, I would've been written up and in a position to lose my job? But God made sure I made it on time and I received a good evaluation and unexpected raise. My boss told me that starting today, I had a clean slate (tardy free). God is good!

What *simple things* could the devil be doing in your life to distract you from your life's purpose?

_____

_____

_____

_____

_____

DAY 46

DAY 46

Stephan:

Alexis makes me so happy and I am proud to be her man. She always goes out of her way to make sure I feel appreciated.

Lately, I've caught myself just staring at her with admiration. I am going to take her out tonight and show her a good time. We are one and the same, so I always know exactly what to do to put a smile on her face.

What I like most about Alexis is that she appreciates the little things. She is just as happy with flowers and a card as she is when I surprise her with diamond earrings. Tonight I am taking her to Chipotle and then we are hitting the movies! We love splitting the bowl and talking as we get full off of our two-for-one special! As she picked dinner, I got to choose the movie. Hopefully, she doesn't fall asleep on my choice of film.

DAY 46

Alexis:

I don't think couples should ever stop dating. We absolutely love it! It keeps us out of a complacent routine.

We both try to throw surprises in, which is always hard as we still finish each other's sentences and practically have all the same ideas. I enjoy getting dolled up and spending time out on the town with Stephan! Showing him off and making sure he feels good about himself is always fun!

I must admit that we have made adjustments to our dating style since we've committed ourselves to celibacy. Some of the changes have been more frustrating than others, but they're like second nature to me now. I don't even think about how I can't wear bandage dresses or braless tops. I just throw on something cute and keep it moving because I don't want to tease Stephan by wearing revealing clothes. This is the type of consideration that true love demonstrates.

> **ROAMANS 14:21** It is good neither to eat flesh, nor to drink wine, nor any thing whereby thy brother stumbleth, or is offended, or is made weak.

In the past, I would've ordered a piña colada or glass of wine, but alcohol triggers my mind and can sometimes have my thoughts all the way in left field. Knowing my triggers helps me prevent mistakes. We have to continue loving our partners God's way, even when it's inconvenient and He will bless us for it.

DAY 47

DAY 47

Stephan:

S ingleness is a blessing. There's no reason to rush marriage because we have fear of waiting. God will bless us for being patient.

We won't find contentment in marriage if we can't be content and obedient during our single season. Marriage is a gift and we won't be in alignment with our assignment if we let the devil trick us into believing that we are ready for something that God hasn't called us to do.

People will try to convince us that we should rush to the courthouse and tie the knot instead of going through the acts of celibacy and embracing an engagement.

I stand strong in believing that there is a purpose behind the commitment to wait. We can only wait on God and move to the next level when He instructs us to do so. That time can come in a week, a month, a year or longer. We can't allow our friends to advise us when we've already given our relationship to God. The wrong counsel can lead us out of His will and then we are back at square one.

Remember that our obedience is for God, not a marriage. We are living a pure life because that's what we are supposed to do.

Our relationship with Christ should be our main concern; everything and everyone else comes after.

DAY 47

Alexis:

As we continue on this journey, let's not forget where we came from. Let's not forget that God's grace and mercy allowed us to be where we are today.

Let's not act like saints who never sinned, because a judgmental Christian cannot win souls and that's what we've been assigned to do. When God tells us to share our testimony and preach the messages that He gives us, we have to do it free of judgment.

Our work has been cut out for us since long before we were born. We weren't randomly placed on this road; He planned for us to be here. If we don't rise to our calling and complete the work the way He has asked us to do it, someone else will rise to the occasion.

When the enemy can't destroy us, he tries to distract us and we can't let him win! There isn't a devil in hell that can tear down what God is building up. Stay committed and stay faithful!

DAY 48

DAY 48

Stephan:

What we do in private shows God who we really are. This isn't the time to fall into a lust trap. When the going gets tough, cry out to God and ask Him to keep you.

We are going to stay free of unhealthy desires that lead to bad actions. We aren't sexual addicts; we don't need to watch anything and we don't need to do anything. In the name of Jesus, we are taken care of and we declare that we will remain celibate until marriage.

Falling short isn't an option; we've come too far. I can't lay with and cuddle up to Alexis like I used to do and allow my hands to travel below her waist when she hugs me or greets me with a kiss. Today I am reminding myself that this way of love is preparing me for an amazing marriage with the woman of my dreams. In the meantime, I will continue loving God and fulfilling the call to love all people without exclusion.

DAY 48

Alexis:

As I've been reading and learning from my pastor and brothers and sisters in Christ, I've learned that forcing a relationship outside of God's will can still work but that doesn't mean that you're walking in alignment. It just means that you are doing what you want to do and you are muting God's voice.

We can't mold our boyfriends into Boaz. We can't make them be the men whom God put on Earth for us. We can't try to raise a man into Christ and expect to receive all of the blessings God has for us.

Sometimes we walk in circles around our destiny because we settle for what's good with haste instead of seeking God and waiting for His very best.

I tell you this: As a woman of God, more women are going to cling to you. They may want what you have and seek your advice concerning their love lives. Personally, I LOVE love! I want everyone to find the love of his or her life and live happily ever after. Being a matchmaker excites me and I find joy in hooking people up, but that isn't always wise. I had to lay that to rest because it is very dangerous.

One of my girlfriends has been single for years. She's been celibate longer than me. She's degreed, beautiful and would make an amazing wife, in my opinion. Can you believe that we spent hours trying to hook her up with different guys? We were on social media for hours stalking dudes' Instagram pages before I snapped out of it and advised her to continue waiting on God. It was so hard because I want her to find a man and be happy, but I also want her to stay within the will of God.

We must be able to identify, especially in the heat of the moment, when we are misleading our friends or encouraging them to do something that isn't wise. Although God is taking us to the next level, we have to remember where we were. The best thing we can do for our single friends is to pray for them and assure them that being single is a blessing and that their partners will come when God sees fit.

MARRIAGE

The idea of spending the rest of your life with someone who loves God and loves you is exciting. Knowing that love is more than sex is relieving. That eliminates sexual addictions, confusion between love and a soul tie, physical attraction versus mental attraction and so on. All we can see is a happy life ahead of us and we can't wait to finally live out our dreams. But we have to be patient.

One month, one year or even one decade of celibacy doesn't mean that we should run off and get married without seeking God's wisdom and blessing. Continuing on our celibacy journey until God calls us to marriage will strengthen our relationship and take us to the next level spiritually.

During this season, patience is truly a virtue. We don't want to become exasperated complainers and end up walking into something that we aren't ordained to deal with. We can't walk around anxious because we are saving ourselves for marriage. That isn't what this is.

We are saving ourselves for Jesus: right now we are connecting with Him, doing what we are instructed to do to be in alignment and walking in the will of God.

Realizing that the devil sends signs, just as Jesus does, is vital. The false prophet works to destroy families, friendships and relationships. He will try to sway us with things that are appealing to the eye and our flesh. His advertisements will lead us into a realm of darkness if we aren't careful.

Right now, we may be eager to move onto marriage. That is

understandable and something to celebrate as we move closer to our goal. But don't let your eagerness allow the devil to win.

In due season, our hopes and dreams will be brought to fruition and the process will be seamless if God leads the way. He will guide us to the light and bless us with peace and everlasting love.

> **HEBREWS 13:4** Marriage is honourable in all, and the bed undefiled: but whoremongers and adulterers God will judge.

DAY 49

DAY 49

Stephan:

Satan is busy! He's in the workplace, the classroom, the house and the car. I am doing my best to stay prayed up, especially when it seems as though more things are going wrong than right. I believe that is when God is getting ready to make a move. During these times, I love to pray and assure myself that God never puts more on us than we can bear.

I've made it to Day 49 of journaling and consistently working on my relationship with God. I am going to spoil myself with a box of pizza and catch up on some sports tonight. Alexis is studying and, after a long day of work, I can use some guy time!

I encourage you to treat yourself as well. Sometimes we get to the point where we want to give up everything we've been praying for. Let's keep our faith strong and continue being faithful; soon we will bear fruit. God works in mysterious ways.

DAY 49

Alexis:

When Stephan and I began dating, I didn't use curse words and I was doing a good job keeping it together. I eventually stopped considering cursing a bad habit and now I struggle with profanity.

I know that God's vision for me will not come to fruition if I don't control my tongue. Sis, if Satan is trying to take over your tongue like I've allowed him to catch hold of mine, please pray with me:

Dear Father God,

I thank You for another opportunity to live life and work for Your kingdom. God, I come to You, asking You to loose my tongue and mind from profanity. I bind every curse word, negative thought, gossip and discouraging word.

I pray for a supernatural force field to wash my mouth and give me a renewed mind. God, allow me to think and pray before I part my lips, for I am a reflection of Your kingdom. Take control over my dialogue and construct my conversation. Break the routine of my natural responses and allow me to think before I speak, oh God.

I know that this life change is possible through You; I am declaring that I am not the same.

I love You, God! Thank You, Jesus, for Your blessing!

Amen.

He inhabits the praise of His people so we can put praise on this prayer and continue living through Him. It is done!

DAY 50

DAY 50

Stephan:

> **MATTHEW 21:22** And all things, whatsoever ye shall ask in prayer, believing, ye shall receive.

This ties into my thoughts and feelings from yesterday. The vital part of this scripture is prayer. I cannot stress enough to you the value of prayer. Over the last 50 days of our journey, if I had to attribute our success to one thing, it would undoubtedly be prayer.

I heard some powerful words yesterday regarding the story of Daniel and the lions' den. We all wonder why the lions did not destroy Daniel in the lions' den.

Daniel's faith was so audacious that even through adversity, he remained in the Spirit in his walk with God. The lions did not desire to consume Daniel because he remained faithful, praying and believing that God would bring him out of any situation, big or small.

Had Daniel been weak in his faith, he would have given up worship and prayer because of his present situation in a den full of ferocious lions, the way the majority of us handle such adversity in our lives. With a lack of trust in God, he would

216

have undoubtedly been destroyed. But because God is so good and it was in His will for Daniel to stay alive, that's exactly what happened.

I do not know what lions you are facing right now in your personal life but, as for my walk with God, it is essential that I spend more time in the spirit and not let my natural flesh cause me to waver in my faith. I rest knowing my God is intentional and he will always take care of me,

DAY 50

Alexis:

My life is continuing to change and I am proud of my growth and intimacy with God. At this point, I thank God for my Christian friends. I've made it this far as a result of prayer and a partner who is on the same page, but my friends have also held me accountable. Their commitment to my walk means a lot to me because it's hard to find friends who don't treat sin like an unashamed reality.

I am proud to say that I have a solid group of girlfriends who don't ignore convictions and make excuses for their actions. We acknowledge that the wages of sin is death (Romans 6:23). We know that we have to listen to God's voice and praise Him for the conviction of sin because, without it, there wouldn't be salvation.

I encourage you to join forces and fellowship with loved ones who have opened their eyes to sin and opened their hearts to receive His grace without taking it for granted. We are only here in the flesh to fulfill our God-given purpose. It is time to get off the fence and choose the right side, the right master. The key to continuing with this life-changing decision is to surround ourselves with positive influences. We all know that bad company corrupts good character (1 Corinthians 15:33).

PARTING WORDS

Making this life change and practicing celibacy has allowed us to break generational curses, inspire other Christians and please God all in the same breath.

When times get tough, we think about all that God has done for us. We know that we have a purpose to fulfill and that this is the beginning of us walking into our destiny.

Marriage is the ultimate goal, but before we get there, we have to practice obedience. If a man cannot submit to God, he is not ready to be responsible for his household. Right now our assignment is to hold each other accountable and to stay rooted in the Word.

True love and healthy marriage will fall in place when it's time, but that doesn't mean that we need to look for our significant other to please us in ways that only God has access to. If we do so, we will always have to depend on them for the joy that only God can provide.

As we move forward in this journey, we will continue growing in Christ. We know that this hardship will bring us the greatest opportunity for glory and teach us to put our faith in God. It is our prayer and deepest desire to remain celibate until after we vow to love one another for the rest of our lives before our families and God.

Hopefully, we are on this ride with our future spouse. But if not, we have transformed our sinful love into the love that God intended for us to have in the beginning.

We know that the greatest gift we can give our loved ones is to know that we are saved in the event that we face an untimely death. It is imperative that we recognize sin for what it is and remember what God says about it. A lot of us believe that sex won't send us to hell, but as we now know, it will. His word is the truth and we live for His purpose.

As we continue to make peace with our past, let's remember to do the best we can to do what's righteous. That's all God wants, for it is He who knows the secrets of our hearts (Psalm 44:21).

ROAMANS 12: I beseech you therefore, brethren, by the mercies of God, that ye present your bodies a living sacrifice, holy, acceptable unto God, which is your reasonable service.

2 And be not conformed to this world: but be ye transformed by the renewing of your mind, that ye may prove what is that good, and acceptable, and perfect, will of God.

CELIBACY
After
SEX

Made in the USA
Monee, IL
05 March 2020